Faithfulness
Bible Story Puzzles

Lessons from Hannah, Esther, Ruth, and Naomi

by
Enelle Eder

Carson-Dellosa Publishing Company, Inc.
Greensboro, North Carolina

It is the mission of Carson-Dellosa Christian Publishing to create the highest-quality Scripture-based children's products that teach the Word of God, share His love and goodness, assist in faith development, and glorify His Son, Jesus Christ.

". . . teach me your ways so I may know you. . . ."
Exodus 33:13

To my granddaughter Victoria,
May you show faithfulness and strength like
these Old Testament women.

Credits

Editor. . . . . Kathie Szitas
Inside Illustrations. . . . . Dave Schimmell
Cover Design . . . . Van Harris
Cover Illustration . . . . Marci McAdam

ISBN: 978-1-60022-518-5

Table of Contents

Hannah

Sad Hannah 4

Hannah's Prayer 5

Hannah's Baby Boy 6

Hannah's Promise 7

A Promise Fulfilled 8

Samuel's Robe 9

Whole-Group Activities 10

Esther

Beautiful Esther 12

Queen Esther 13

Trouble for God's Jewish People 14

Esther's Plan 15

An Angry King 16

Esther's Request 17

Whole-Group Activities 18

Ruth and Naomi

Naomi Leaves Home 20

Sad Naomi 21

Loving Ruth 22

Gathering Grain 23

Boaz 24

God Blesses Ruth 25

Naomi's Decision 26

Ruth Marries Boaz 27

A Royal Family 28

Whole-Group Activities 29

Hannah, Esther, Ruth, and Naomi Review 32

Caution: Before completing any food activity, ask families' permission and inquire about students' food allergies and religious or other food preferences.

Sad Hannah

Hannah was sad because she did not have a baby. Every year she went with her husband, Elkanah, to the temple to worship. Elkanah's other wife, Peninnah, went, too. She had many children and teased Hannah. **Even though Hannah was sad, she was still faithful to Elkanah and to God.**

Find and circle 5 things in picture 1 that are missing from picture 2.

Picture 1

Picture 2

"Peninnah teased Hannah to make her angry. She did it because the Lord had kept Hannah from having children." 1 Samuel 1:6

4

Hannah's Prayer

One year, when Hannah went to the temple to pray, she was so overcome with sadness that when she prayed her lips moved but no words came out. Eli, the priest, thought she was drunk. He scolded Hannah, but she said, "No, I am not drunk; I am sad because I don't have a baby." Eli told her to go in peace and that the Lord had heard her prayers. **Hannah wasn't sad anymore. She faithfully believed Eli and God.**

Circle the words from the word bank in the word search.

Word Bank		
PRAY	SAD	BABY

R I V X Z Q
A P T E L P
S S F Z U R
A O N I E A
D L B A B Y

"Eli answered, 'Go in peace. May the God of Israel give you what you have asked him for.'" 1 Samuel 1:17

5

Hannah's Baby Boy

So Hannah went home, and this time her heart felt light. In a short time, she had a baby boy. She named him a name that means, "I asked the Lord for him." **Hannah trusted God. God answered Hannah's faithful prayers.**

Do you know what Hannah named her little boy? Match the letters with the pictures. Then, write the letters on the lines below to find out the name of Hannah's son.

"After some time, Hannah became pregnant. She had a baby boy.
She said, 'I asked the Lord for him.' So she named him Samuel." 1 Samuel 1:20

Hannah's Promise

When Hannah prayed and asked for a son, she made a promise to God. She promised to give her son back to serve the Lord all the days of his life. **Hannah was faithful to the Lord.**

Can you help Hannah keep her promise by taking Samuel to the temple?

Start

Finish

"She made a promise to him. She said, '. . . . Don't forget about me! Please give me a son!
If you do, I'll give him back to you. Then he will serve you all the days of his life.'" 1 Samuel 1:11

A Promise Fulfilled

When Samuel was old enough, Hannah brought him back to the temple and left him there with Eli, the priest. Samuel served God at the temple. **Hannah was faithful to her promise.**

Find 5 things in this picture that are wrong. Circle them and then color the picture.

"I prayed for this child. The Lord has given me what I asked him for. So now I'm giving him to the Lord. As long as he lives he'll be given to the Lord."   1 Samuel 1:27-28

Samuel's Robe

Hannah did not forget about her son. She loved Samuel very much. Each year when she and Elkanah came to the temple to worship, Hannah brought a new robe she had made for Samuel. **Hannah was faithful to Samuel.**

Follow the code and color all the shapes in the picture below.

1 = red   2 = yellow   3 = green   4 = blue

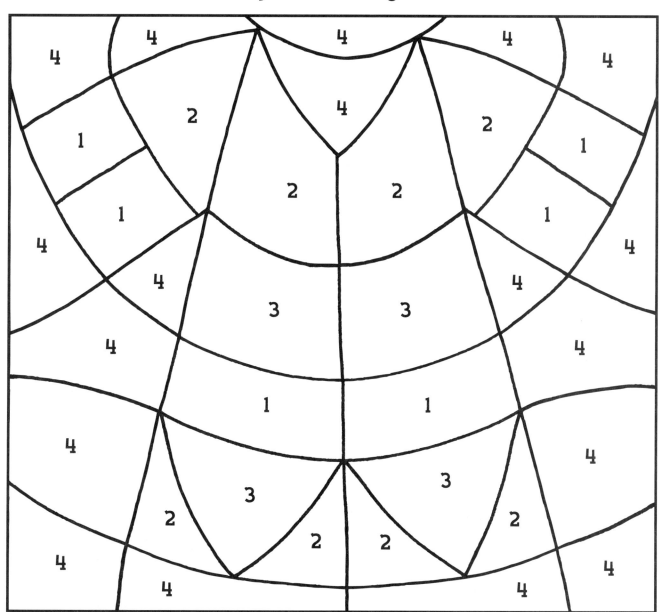

"Each year his mother made him a little robe. She took it to him when she went up to Shiloh with her husband. She did it when her husband went to offer the yearly sacrifice." 1 Samuel 2:19

Hannah
Whole-Group Activities

Game
Robe Race
Read 1 Samuel 2:19–20. Review with the children the story of Hannah and Samuel. Then, tell them they are going to play a game with robes to remind them of Hannah's faithfulness to Samuel.

Items Needed: 2 child-sized robes with tie belts, masking tape, and an open area

Prepare: Place a strip of masking tape on the floor at each end of the area. Designate one side as "A" and one as "B." Divide the children into two teams. Put one half of each team on each side. Have the children stand in lines behind the masking tape.

To Play: Give a robe to the first child from each team on side "A." Tell them they must put on the robe and tie the belt, then race over to side "B," take it off, and hand it to the next teammate. The teammate must put on the robe, tie it, and race over to side "A." Have the children continue until all teammates have put on a robe and exchanged sides.

Craft
Samuel's Robe
Say, "Samuel showed his faithfulness to God by staying with the priest Eli and serving in the temple. His mother faithfully made a robe for Samuel and brought it to him every year." Tell the children they are going to make robes like the one Hannah might have made for Samuel.

Items Needed: large grocery bags (one for each child), markers or crayons, stickers, scraps of fabric, scraps of colorful construction paper, glue, scissors

Prepare: Open each bag and cut a slit up the middle of the front. Then cut a hole in the bag's bottom that is large enough for a child's head to fit through. Cut out an armhole on each side.

Let the children decorate their robes any way they like. After the decorations have dried, encourage the children to wear the robes home and tell their parents the story of Hannah and Samuel.

Hannah
Whole-Group Activities

Snack
Sweet Robes

Here is a treat the children can help make.

Items Needed: people-shaped cookie (like a gingerbread man) for each child, can of frosting, wax paper, sandwich bags, scissors

Prepare: Put a tablespoon of frosting in the corner of a sandwich bag. Give each child a cookie on a square of wax paper and a bag of frosting. Then, snip off the corner and have them squeeze out the frosting to draw a robe on the cookie.

Pray: *Thank You, Lord, for being faithful to us in every way. Help us to be faithful to You, and faithful to the promises that we make to our family and friends. Amen.*

Beautiful Esther

Esther was a beautiful, young Jewish girl. She was raised by her cousin Mordecai because she didn't have any parents. When King Xerxes was looking for a new queen, he brought Esther to the palace. When Mordecai heard this, he told Esther not to tell anyone that she was Jewish. **Esther was faithful to Mordecai.**

Follow the paths from the crowns and write the letters on the lines below. Then, color the 2 matching crowns.

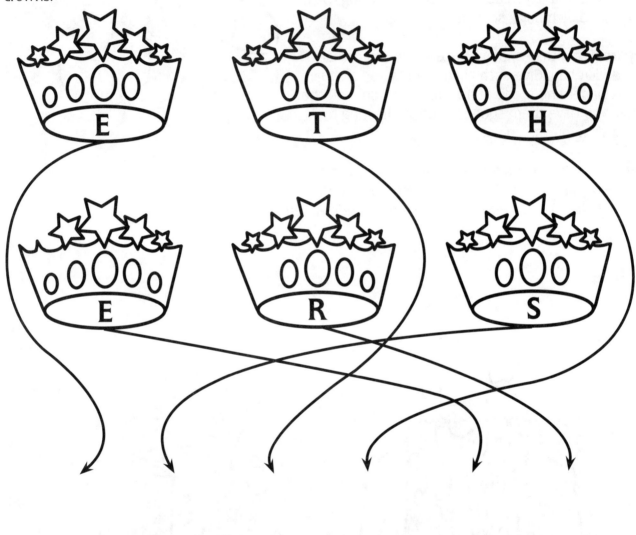

____ ____ ____ ____ ____ ____

"Esther hadn't told anyone who her people were. She hadn't talked about her family. That's because Mordecai had told her not to."   Esther 2:10

Queen Esther

When Esther came before King Xerxes, he fell in love with her immediately. The king put a crown on her head and made Esther his queen. While Esther lived in the palace and Mordecai lived outside the palace walls, **she faithfully kept the secret that she was Jewish.**

Draw a picture of the queen and king inside the crown frame below.

"The king liked Esther more than he liked any of the other women. She pleased him more than any of the other virgins. So he put a royal crown on her head." Esther 2:17

Trouble for God's Jewish People

While Esther lived in the palace, Mordecai found out that an evil man, named Haman, had gotten the king to sign a law saying that all the Jewish people would be killed. Mordecai sent word to Esther that she must talk to the king for the sake of her people. **Esther was faithful to her people.**

Use the color code to color the picture of king Xerxes and Haman below.

◗ = blue   ◆ = yellow   ✦ = red   ✳ = purple

"... He told him to try and get her to go to the king. He wanted her to beg
for mercy. He wanted her to make an appeal to the king for her people." Esther 4:8

Esther's Plan

Esther knew that if the king found out that she was Jewish, she might be killed. But Esther believed that God would be with her. So she made a plan to talk to the king. She fasted for 3 days before she went to see the king, and she asked Mordecai to do the same. **Esther was faithful to God.**

Help Queen Esther find her way through the maze to get to the king.

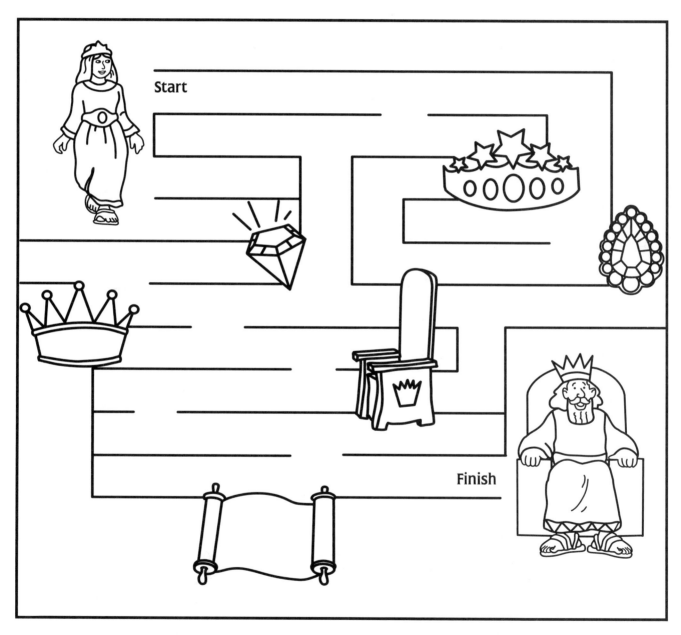

"'Don't eat or drink anything for three days. Don't do it night or day.
I and my attendants will fast just as you do. Then I'll go to the king.
I'll do it even though it's against the law. And if I have to die, I'll die.'" Esther 4:16

Faithfulness PK-K • CD-204064

An Angry King

Esther invited the king to a banquet meal. She told the king that her people had been sold to be killed. The king was angry and said, "Who would do such a thing?" Esther told him that Haman had done it. The king ordered Haman hanged. **Esther remained faithful to her people.**

Find the objects hidden in the picture below.

"King Xerxes asked Queen Esther, 'Who is the man who
has dared to do such a thing? And where is he?'" Esther 7:5

Esther's Request

Esther asked the king to write a new law that would overrule the old law against the Jewish people. The king loved Esther very much, so he made the new law. **Esther was faithful to God and to her people.**

Find and circle the words from the word bank in the word-search puzzle below.

Word Bank

KING
RULE
LOVE
NEW

K	I	N	G	L
A	C	E	D	O
M	J	W	R	V
P	R	U	L	E

"The king asked, 'What is it, Queen Esther? What do you want?
I'll give it to you. I'll even give you up to half of my kingdom.'" Esther 5:3

Esther
Whole-Group Activities

Game

Crown Exchange Game

Remind the children that even after the king put a beautiful crown on Esther's head, she remained faithful to God and to her people. Tell them that they are going to play a game using a crown, too.

Items Needed: glue; scissors; stapler; sheets of red, blue, green, and yellow construction paper; stickers; gemstones; glitter; etc. Make one simple (nondecorated) crown from the construction paper. Make an equal number of crowns of each color.

To Play: Distribute one crown to each child, and have the children sit in a circle. Choose a child to be the leader. Have the leader say this rhyme:

I'm like a queen/king. (Change genders each time.)
Just see my crown.
Now change with a friend.
Then sit down.

The leader then calls out two colors (for example, blue, red). The children wearing either of those colors must jump up and exchange their crowns for crowns of the other color called and then sit back down. After playing long enough for each child to have a turn, let the children decorate their crowns.

Craft

Clothes Pin Queens

Read Esther 7:1–3 to the children. Remind them how brave Esther was to go before the king and speak for her people. Tell them they are going to make Queen Esther puppets.

Items Needed: clothespin puppet pattern (page 19) for each child, mini clip-style clothespins, white glue, crayons, scissors

To Make: Let the children color and cut out the clothespin puppet pattern. Assist as needed with the cutting. Fold the puppet inward on the center fold line where indicated (illustration A). Fold back the lower half of the pattern on the second fold line (illustration B). Put a drop of glue on the inside of the pincher part of the clothespin (illustration C). Clip the clothespin to the back center fold of the pattern. Let the puppet dry (illustration D).

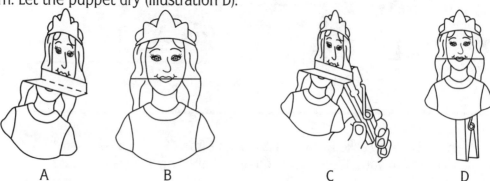

A   B   C   D

18

Esther
Whole-Group Activities

Practice using your puppet to say this little speech:

Oh, my king, so brave and strong!
Something here is very wrong.
And if you really love me so,
Please rule to let my people go!

Snack

Crown Sandwich The children will enjoy making and eating this healthy, fun snack.

Items Needed: 1 slice of whole wheat bread for each child, cheese spread, raisins, cherry halves (or other fruit bits), plastic knives, and cardboard crown templates (1 per 2 children)

Prepare: Prior to class, cut crown templates from cardboard to fit on a slice of bread. Group the children in twos and encourage them to share the crown template and plastic knives.

To Make: Lay the crown template on a piece of bread. Using the plastic knife, cut around the template to create a crown from the bread. Spread each slice with cheese spread. Guide the children in decorating their crown snacks with the other food items.

Pray: *Lord, thank You for always being faithful to us. Help us to be brave in our faith and to turn to You, just like Queen Esther did, when we are afraid or there is trouble in our lives. Amen.*

Clothespin Puppet Pattern

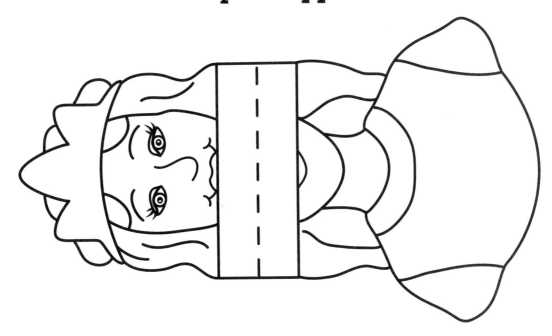

Naomi Leaves Home

Naomi lived in Bethlehem with her husband Elimelech and their two sons. There was a famine, and they had very little to eat. Naomi's husband decided to move to a different part of the country, called Moab, where they had plenty of food. **Faithfully, Naomi followed her husband to Moab.**

Follow the path from start to finish. Each time you find a letter, write it in order on the blank below the puzzle to find a word to describe Naomi.

"There wasn't enough food in the land of Judah. So a man went to live in the country of Moab for a while. He was from Bethlehem in Judah. His wife and two sons went with him." Ruth 1:1

Sad Naomi

While in Moab, both of Naomi's sons got married. Some time later, Naomi's husband died, and then her sons died also. Naomi was very sad. She heard that there was food in Bethlehem again. She decided to take both her daughters-in-law, Ruth and Orpah, and go back home. They prepared to go to Bethlehem. **Naomi was faithful to her family.**

Follow the maze to get Naomi, Ruth, and Orpah back to Bethlehem.

"She left the place where she had been living. Her two daughters-in-law went with her. They started out on the road that would take them back to the land of Judah." Ruth 1:7

Loving Ruth

When they had started the journey, Naomi urged her daughters-in-law to go back to their parents' homes. Orpah went back, but Ruth would not go. She said, "I will go wherever you go. I will stay with you the rest of my life. I will serve your God." **Ruth was faithful to Naomi.**

Color the picture using the color code.

1 = red   2 = blue   3 = green   4 = yellow   5 = brown

"Naomi realized that Ruth had made up her mind to go with her. So she stopped
trying to make her go back. The two women continued on their way." Ruth 1:18–19

Gathering Grain

When Ruth and Naomi reached Bethlehem, they had no money. It was harvest time, so Naomi told Ruth to take a basket and walk along the edges of the field and pick up the grain that fell there. Ruth did as Naomi told her. **Ruth was faithful to Naomi.**

Find 5 stalks of grain hidden in the picture.

"So Ruth went out and began to pick up grain. She worked in the
fields behind those who were cutting and gathering the grain." Ruth 2:3

Boaz

The field where Ruth picked up grain belonged to a kind man named Boaz. He was a relative of Naomi's late husband. When he saw Ruth, he asked the workers who she was and they told him. **Boaz noticed how faithfully Ruth worked.**

Look at the pictures. Circle the 5 items in picture 1 that are not in picture 2.

Picture 1

Picture 2

"As it turned out, she was working in a field that
belonged to Boaz. He was from the family of Elimelech."   Ruth 2:3

God Blesses Ruth

Boaz found out that Ruth was taking care of Naomi. He was pleased. He gave her water to drink while she worked, and he made sure that she had extra grain each day. **Through Boaz, God blessed Ruth for her faithfulness.**

Find 7 water pitchers hidden in the picture.

"'May the Lord reward you for what you have done.'" Ruth 2:12

Naomi's Decision

Even though Ruth and Naomi had plenty to eat, they were still very poor. Naomi decided she must sell her husband's land. When Boaz heard this, he declared, "I will buy the land, and I will marry Ruth." **God had a plan for Ruth's life, and Naomi was faithful to God's plan.**

Color the picture that is different from the others.

"'Today you are witnesses. You have seen that I have bought land from Naomi. I have bought all of the property that had belonged to Elimelech, Kilion and Mahlon. I've also taken Ruth, who is from Moab, to become my wife.'" Ruth 4: 9–10

Ruth Marries Boaz

Ruth and Boaz were married, and soon they had a baby son named Obed. Naomi loved little Obed and he brought joy to her life again. **God rewarded Naomi's faithfulness.**

Circle 5 items in the picture that do not belong.

"So Boaz got married to Ruth. She became his wife. . . . And she had a son." Ruth 4:13

A Royal Family

When Ruth's son Obed grew up, he had a son named Jesse, and Jesse grew up to have a son named David. Ruth was David's great-grandmother. Many years later, Jesus was born into the family line of David. **Ruth's faithfulness was rewarded.**

Color the shapes red that have a † in them. Color the shapes blue that have a ♡ in them to find a relative of Ruth.

"The women who were living there said, 'Naomi has a son.' They named him Obed. He was the father of Jesse. Jesse was the father of David." Ruth 4:17

28

Ruth and Naomi
Whole-Group Activities

Craft

Basket Pouches

Read Ruth 2:2–3 to the children. Talk about how Ruth went to the fields to pick up pieces of fallen grain so that she and Naomi would have food to eat. Say, "Ruth was faithful to Naomi." Tell them they are going to make a basket pouch like Ruth may have worn to gather grain.

Items Needed: brown grocery bags (one for every two children), scissors, stapler, paper punch, yarn, and crayons or markers

Prepare: Cut an 11½" (29.21 cm) square from a grocery bag for each child. Cut 72" (182.88 cm) of yarn for each child. Fold the yarn in half, and tie a knot in both ends.

To Make:

1. Have the children fold both side points of the paper square in to overlap. (Step 1)
2. Fold the bottom point up and fold it over the two side points. Staple together. (Step 2)
3. Fold the top point back and punch two holes, an inch apart. (Step 3)
4. Thread the yarn through the holes. (Step 3)
5. Decorate the pouch with crayons or markers. Tie the pouches around the children's waists.

Step 1	Step 2	Step 3
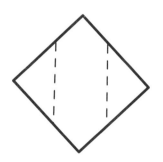	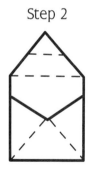	

Snack

Items Needed: wheat cereal, rice cakes, popcorn, paper plates or bowls.

Prepare: Place rice cakes, wheat cereal and popcorn on separate paper plates or bowls for the children to gather and place in their pouches for snack time.

Pray: *Thank You, Father, for providing for us every day. Thank You for being faithful to us. Teach us to be faithful to You in all ways. Amen.*

Ruth and Naomi
Whole-Group Activities

Craft

Family Trees

Read Ruth 4:16–17 and Luke 2:4. Talk to the children about having a family tree. Explain that a family tree is where their family members' names are recorded. Tell them: "Ruth would have been on Jesus' family tree. We are going to make a family tree to record the names in your family."

Items Needed: red and green construction paper, scissors, copy of the tree and apple pattern (page 31). One tree pattern on green construction paper for each child.

Approximately 5–6 apple patterns per child on red construction paper. Have extra on hand for those who may need them.

Prepare: Before class, make templates of the tree and apple patterns (page 31).

1. Fold a sheet of green construction paper in half. Place the tree pattern on the fold and trace around it. Cut out the tree.

2. Trace and cut out apples from red construction paper.

3. Write the names of as many family members as each child can remember on the apples. (Encourage them to try and think of their grandparents' names–even if the child just says, "Gramma" or another nickname.)

4. Cut V-shaped slits in the tree and place the apples in the slits. Write "(child's last name) Family" down the trunk.

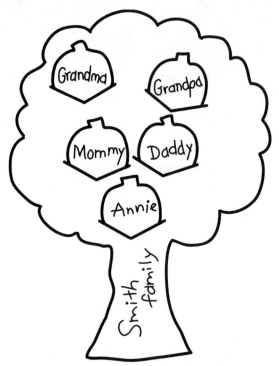

Snack

Apple-Licious

Items needed: several apples, enough for several apple slices per child; apple juice; napkins; small paper cups

Prepare: Slice the apples into small sections. Place several slices on a napkin for each child. Serve apple juice in paper cups.

Pray: *Father, thank You for our families. Help us to be faithful to our families and faithful to others in our promises, words, and actions. Amen.*

Ruth and Naomi
Tree and Apple Patterns

Hannah, Esther, Ruth and Naomi
Review

To be faithful means to be loyal, true, and trustworthy. Hannah, Esther, Ruth, and Naomi showed that they were faithful to God and to their families. **We can be faithful, too, by reading God's Word and obeying it, by serving others, and by showing love in every situation.**

Match the pictures of each faithful woman on the left with the pictures on the right of something from her story.

"A faithful man will be richly blessed." Proverbs 28:20